Everyday Faith

SHARI GUILFOILE

ISBN: 978-0-9889053-0-6

"We must become the change we want to see in the world."

-- Mahatma Gandhi

.

CONTENTS

FORGIVENESS

PERSPECTIVE

PRAYER

PURPOSE

RELATIONSHIPS

SERVICE

TRANSFORMATION

TRUST

.

"Pray not for easier lives; pray to be stronger men."

-- John F. Kennedy

Don't Ask Why, Ask How

When tragedy strikes, people often ask: *Why does God let bad things happen?* This question has been debated forever. Some people believe God has a plan for each one of us, and events, good and bad, happen for a reason. Others believe God does not direct the tragedies that occur in this world. Bad things just happen; people make evil choices, and God is as outraged and saddened as we are when these things happen.

The point is, we don't know why bad things happen, nor do we need to know. Dwelling on why something happened takes the focus off the question you should be asking. Instead of asking why, you need to ask how: how you can get through a difficult situation, or how you can help someone else get through a difficult situation. Focusing on how to move forward will lead to strength, courage and wisdom during difficult times.

"God never shows us something we aren't ready to understand. Instead, He lets us see what we need to see, when we need to see it. He will plant our feet on the path that's best for us, but it's up to us to do the walking."

– Immaculee Ilibagiza, Rwandan genocide survivor

Flashlights, Not Floodlights

Why doesn't God show you the big picture of what He wants you to do with your life? Possibly because if you saw the big picture, you might feel overwhelmed and may even be deterred from the path He wants you to take.

Think about it. If God had told Mother Theresa she would eventually have over 100,000 volunteers serving the poor on six continents, and that she would even receive the Nobel Peace Prize, she may have first hired a consulting firm to begin developing her strategic plan! Instead, she just started taking care of the poor one by one, and God took care of the rest.

Remember, God doesn't give you a floodlight, instead He gives you a flashlight – just enough light to see a few steps ahead. You need to trust He knows what He is doing, where He is leading you, and that He will be with you every step of the way. Then you just need to start taking some steps.

"I have missed over 9000 shots, I have lost almost 300 games, 26 times I've been trusted to take the game winning shot and missed. I've failed over and over and over in my life, and that is why I succeed."

-- Michael Jordan, acclaimed as best basketball player of all time

Gifts in Disguise

Obviously, you do not like to fail. Nor do you like to see those you care about fail. But failure is often a gift in disguise. Why?

Most spiritual leaders would agree that after the age of 35 or so, there is very little we learn from our successes. But we could probably write novels about what we learned from our mistakes. So how do you tap into this goldmine of wisdom?

First, view failure or defeat as a gift. And what do you do with a gift? You open it, examine it, spend some time with it, and then find the nuggets of gold that it contains. If you cannot find a nugget, ask God to show you where it is. Do not give up; there is always something valuable to be found.

Once found, reflect on it, maybe write it down, and say it out loud, preferably to someone close to you. Let it seep into your soul because if you do, it *will* shape and mold you in very beneficial ways.

"Everyone says forgiveness is a lovely idea, until they have something to forgive."

-- C.S. Lewis, author, lay theologian

No Exceptions

Forgiveness. Sounds simple, doesn't it? But as simple as it sounds, you may still have people in your life who you do not want to forgive, or if you do, you just cannot seem to do it. So are you off the hook if you are able to forgive most of the time? Are you OK in God's eyes if you are withholding forgiveness from only a few people?

What does the Bible say? It says *if we want God to forgive our sins, we must forgive others.* And guess what? It does not include any exceptions.

So how do you forgive when forgiveness is tough? First, recognize that you do not have to deny your feelings, you do not have to accept bad behavior, and you do not need remorse from the person you are forgiving. All you need to do is make a decision to replace your anger or hurt with a feeling of peace. Remember, forgiveness is about y*our* attitude and y*our* emotions, so you do not need anything from someone else to do what God expects from you.

"Courage is not the absence of fear, but rather the judgment that something else is more important than fear."

-- Ambrose Redmoon, author

.

Be Not Afraid

Be not afraid. Many experts say this phrase is mentioned over 300 times in the Bible. Why? Does it mean to trust God when circumstances seem to be crumbling around you? Possibly, but God may be saying something else as well. This phrase may also mean to not fear saying what needs to be said, doing what is uncomfortable to do, and accomplishing what is difficult to achieve.

What kind of fear stops you from doing these things? Fear of rejection? Of being misunderstood? Of not being worthy enough? These kinds of fears are real, and can only be circumvented by your trust in God that you are embarking on whatever it is that He needs you to do.

Do you think Rosa Parks felt fear as she took her seat at the front of the bus? Most likely she did, but she did it anyway because she knew what she was doing was right, it was good, it was needed. Your life is full of situations calling for you to step outside your comfort zone and do the very same thing.

"When a man finds that it is his destiny to suffer, he will have to accept his suffering as his task. His unique opportunity lies in the way in which he bears his burden."

-- Victor Frankl, Holocaust survivor

Place of the Break

My son broke his hand, and after his cast was removed, another x-ray was taken that showed the previously broken bone as being a much brighter and more solid white on the x-ray than all the other bones in his hand. The doctor said the x-ray was typical, because *the place of the break is the place of greatest strength.* That is a profound statement, not as it relates to broken bones, but as it relates to interior brokenness and the spiritual strength that can develop.

You see, whenever you experience a devastating event in your life, a typical first reaction is to be scared, angry, overwhelmed. But very often, after that first reaction, you can find a sense of peace and strength you did not think was possible, *if* you turn to God. If you turn to God, the brokenness you feel inside begins to heal, and your spiritual journey gets a sudden burst of acceleration. Th*e place of the break is the place of greatest strength.*

"The best wines have to be aged in cracked old barrels. And so too does the human soul, which comes to compassion only when there are real cracks, painful ones, in the body and life of the one who carries it."

-- James Hillman, psychologist

Compassion

Most of us tend to be compassionate people, and you probably are as well. But there may be times when you withhold compassion. Why? Because these situations involve people who you believe to be immoral, selfish, or have some other character flaw.

Of course if someone who you deem as selfish or immoral faced a devastating hardship, you would rush to his aid. But what about in your normal, day-to-day dealings with them? Are you as apt to extend kindness and mercy to these people as you are to others?

How *do* you develop compassion for a person who, quite frankly, you really don't care for? One way is simply by recognizing the part of *yourself* that is flawed, and admitting how difficult it is to overcome it. This kind of reflection is not designed to make you feel bad about yourself. It simply helps develop some empathy and compassion for others who, just like yourself, struggle to be all God wants them to be.

"A bend in the road is not the end of the road -- unless you fail to make the turn."

-- Unknown

Turning Points

Turning points are disappointments, failures, and crises that have the power to change your life journey.

Paula D'Arcy knows a thing or two about turning points. One *major* turning point in her life occurred at the hands of a drunk driver, who hit the vehicle in which she, her husband and 21-month-old daughter were traveling. She survived; her husband and daughter did not.

Paula D'Arcy had a choice: she could harden and turn away from her pain, but instead, she chose to open and turn toward it. She let her life, with all of its seemingly unfair turns, teach her and turn her toward the work the world needed her to do, work that has helped people from all corners of the globe, including those in prison and those living in third world countries.

Turning toward your difficulties means asking the question, "What is life trying to help me see?" And it means allowing life to unfold in a way that you perhaps never wanted, but never the less, accept and embrace.

"The more you invest in a marriage, the more valuable it becomes."

– Amy Grant, singer, songwriter, author

Model for Marriage

Have you ever considered that your relationship with your kids could be a model for your relationship with your spouse? Think about it: you nurture your kids, you challenge them, and you forgive them. You probably have high standards, yet you understand when those standards can't be met. As a parent, you give, and give, and give – and amazingly, without any return expectations, you receive incredible love and joy, and *you* become a better person. After all, do you know of any parent who wouldn't claim that raising kids helped them, the parent, become more humble, accepting, loving and forgiving?

Of course your spouse is not as dependent or needy as your kids, but that does not mean the opportunities to give and receive are any less. Marriage probably provides your best opportunity to become the person God wants you to be, if you approach it in a way that you give and give and give to your spouse without any sort of scorecard for what you receive.

"Change your perspective and you change your reality."

-- Unknown

Eternal Horizon

Have you ever seen a two year old break her favorite toy? If you have, you may have witnessed an inconsolable meltdown. After all, most kids do not have the perspective to realize how insignificant and fleeting these kinds of experiences are.

How about you? Do you manage to keep your challenges in perspective? Not challenges that arise from broken toys, but rather from the pains and preoccupations of daily life, which can include broken relationships, strained bank accounts, serious health problems and the like.

Often the only perspective that can heal and console us is to see our lives against an eternal horizon. Our faith tells us that our life here is not the real game, it is more like the pre-game warm-ups to prepare us for the real game. Try to find some people in your life who can help you maintain this perspective, and then become a person of perspective for others.

"Sometimes you have to let go of the life you pictured in order to have the life that God has planned."

-- John Hagee, pastor

God's Way, Not Your Way

Legendary college football coach, Lou Holtz, has been known to say, "If you want to make God laugh, tell Him what *your* plans are." Coach Holtz recounts how all through his early years, he would pray and pray to be a good athlete. But God never answered that prayer. Instead, God put Lou in the coaching field where for over 30 years, he had the pleasure and honor of helping young people become successful. Lou knew he wanted to spend his life in athletics, and he thought he wanted to do that as a player, but God had a much better plan.

God will always answer your prayers, but not always by responding to your initial desire. If He does not give you what you ask for, perhaps you should ask Him what it is that you need. When you learn to listen for God's point of view, you often become receptive to ideas you may have suppressed by your own way of thinking. And just like Lou Holtz, you may find yourself eventually thanking Him for not answering your original request.

"Sometimes our light goes out but is blown into flame by another human being. Each of us owes deepest thanks to those who have rekindled this light."

-- Albert Schweitzer, Nobel Peace Prize winner

Fellowship of Pain

Everyone experiences difficulties in life, and those difficulties did not necessarily come from God. But even before you were born, God knew the adversity you would face, and He did two things: First, He gave you everything you would need to persevere. And second -- and this is the part often overlooked -- He made sure you would have plenty of opportunity to help others who face circumstances just like yours.

Nobel Peace Prize winner Albert Schweitzer had a name for this phenomenon. He called it, "The Fellowship of Those Who Bear the Mark of Pain." If you have experienced difficult physical or emotional pain, then you are a member of this fellowship. Dr. Schweitzer believed that once your pain is extinguished, you are not at liberty to just take up your life as it was before your pain. Instead, you are now part of a fellowship of people whose eyes have been opened, and are therefore called by God to help others.

"We tend to end up as good people, but as people who are not very deep - not bad, just busy; not immoral, just distracted; not lacking in soul, just preoccupied; not disdaining depth, just lacking in practice."

-- Ron Rolheiser, author, speaker, priest

Our Narcotic Culture

Our culture is a powerful narcotic, which can be both good and bad. Good in that a narcotic soothes and protects against brute, raw pain. Our culture has within it all sorts of anesthetics, from medicine to entertainment, to shield you from pain. That can be good, providing it is not a false crutch.

But a narcotic can also be bad, especially when it becomes a way of escaping from reality. It can perpetually insulate you by keeping you so entertained, so preoccupied, and so distracted that you lose focus on the deeper issues of life such as faith, forgiveness, morality, and love.

Who or what makes *you* focus on these deeper thoughts? Whoever or whatever it is, seek it. Make time for it. Schedule it. It will spur your spiritual growth, which is ultimately why you are here.

"The only thing missing in any situation is that which you are not giving."

-- Marianne Williamson, author, speaker

No Magic Wand

Sometimes we have to think carefully about what we are asking God to do.

For years I prayed to God to heal a friend who had a serious health problem. Unfortunately the problem continued. Then I changed my prayer. Instead of asking God to heal Joe, I asked God to *show me what I could do to help heal Joe.* Suddenly, all kinds of information started coming to me about this health problem. I shared this knowledge with Joe, and he is now healed of many of the symptoms he had for years.

Why did it take so long for God to answer my prayer? Because by changing the request from, *"God please heal Joe,"* to *"God, please show ME how to help heal Joe,"* I became much more open to hearing God. God may have tried to show me what I could do when I was asking Him to heal Joe, but I probably wasn't listening because I was relying on God to do the work. Remember, God doesn't use a magic wand – he uses people. And in this case, He was waiting to use me, but had to wait until I was ready to hear Him.

What might God be waiting for you to do?

"Pride gets no pleasure out of having something, only out of having more of it than the next man."

-- C.S. Lewis, lay theologian and author

.

Self-Esteem: Healthy or Not?

Self-esteem is a desirable trait, except when it is derived from comparisons to others. If your self-esteem is dependent on how well you measure up to others, you are eventually in for a big crash. Some day your looks will fade, your abilities will deteriorate, and that promotion you wanted will be given to a younger co-worker. If your self-esteem depends on comparisons to others, you will be devastated when these events occur. But if you are only focused on being the best you can be, you will be largely unaffected.

To get and maintain healthy self-esteem, keep this thought in mind: recognize that any gift you have, anything that you are good at, exists only because God made you that way. Instead of filling your head with thoughts about all the many truly great things about you, dwell on why God made you the way He did. If you figure out the reason, you will feel far greater joy than you ever felt by just being more *'whatever'* than everyone else.

"Faith is not for overcoming obstacles, it is for experiencing them."

-Richard Rohr, ecumenical teacher, speaker, author

Deep Faith?

How do you know if a person has great faith? Can you tell by how often they go to church? How often they pray? By how good they are? Of course many people of great faith attend church often, pray often and live good and moral lives, but do these criteria really tell us how faith-filled a person is?

If you had to identify a single characteristic to signify the depth of a person's faith, it might be how they handle adversity. A person of deep faith takes comfort in the belief that God is always present and in charge. They don't believe God will necessarily step in and fix their problems, but they believe God is always right beside them offering wisdom and strength.

What do you believe about God? Do you simply believe He exists? Or, do you believe He is right there with you, no matter how tough life gets? If you believe and trust He's with you, not only will you be able to handle whatever life throws you, but others will observe your strength. They will want what you have, which is deep and meaningful faith.

"Family is not the place where everything goes well, but it is the place where we live through the furnace of life and are transformed by our day-to-day relationships."

-- Rebecca Laird, author, ordained minister

Family Furnace

Many homes built prior to World War II had coal furnaces. The coal furnace would create warmth in the cold winter months, but every so often, it would backfire, and whoever was tending it at the time would be covered with soot.

The coal furnace is a metaphor for our families. Families provide feelings of warmth and comfort, but there are frequently times when we feel like we just got blasted *by our own soot*, which can actually be beneficial. Realistically, you cannot exist very long within a marriage or family without becoming acutely aware of your own faults. Family is where your weaknesses and vulnerabilities are *supposed* to surface because those are the things you need to work on.

When a coal furnace would backfire, the homeowner would not abandon it. He or she would just clean up the mess and get it working again. That is all God is asking of you as well. When one of your shortcomings becomes painfully obvious, restore any relationships that may have been harmed, and then repair whatever it is about yourself that God wants you to fix.

.

"Most people have come to prefer certain of life's experiences and deny and reject others, unaware of the value of the hidden things that may come wrapped in plain or even ugly paper."

-- Rachel Naomi Remen, M.D., author, speaker

No Pain, No Gain

Nobody wants to have problems in life. That is just simple human nature.

It is also human nature to want inner peace, to feel calm and content. You may tend to believe peace will arrive when your problems depart, but inner peace does not come from resolving your problems. Instead, it comes from cultivating perspective, meaning and wisdom precisely at the time that life deals you a difficult hand. In other words, when you are in pain, that is the time to ask God to give you perspective and wisdom to handle the pain. Sure, you can ask Him to help resolve the problem, but make sure you also ask for peace to deal with the problem. This simple request, combined with a receptive heart and mind, creates the perfect conditions for calm within the storm. Inner peace is a spiritual quality, and most spiritual growth comes from pain.

No pain, no gain.

"You can't connect the dots looking forward, you can only connect them looking backwards."

-- Steve Jobs

Connecting the Dots

Do you know why you have so many fonts on your computer? Steve Jobs said it is because of a series of events in his life that on the surface appear unrelated and insignificant. He said that solely due to an adoption agreement between his birthmother and adoptive parents, he briefly attended college. But because he dropped out, he was able to sit in on a calligraphy class at that college, which happened to be the leading calligraphy school in the country. Later, it was Jobs who insisted on providing a vast array of fonts on Apple computers, and the rest is history.

Right from birth, the picture that began forming of Steve's life looked nothing like what it was to become. But he observed that all the seemingly disconnected events eventually connected, enabling him to revolutionize how we live our lives.

The supposed random events in Steve Jobs' life were brought to him by God, as are the events in your life. Looking forward, the events look rather erratic. But if you have faith to forgo aspects of *your* vision, when you look backward, a picture emerges. And with an artist's signature in the corner that says *God*, it is a picture every bit as consequential as the one painted for Steve Jobs.

"Resentment is like taking a poison and waiting for the other person to die."

-- Malachy McCourt, actor, author

The High Road

How do you respond to people who make your blood boil: people who oppose your ideas, misconstrue what you say, treat others badly? You have a few of those people in your life, don't you?

Are you sympathetic when these people misunderstand you? Are you warm and gracious in the face of bitterness? Are you forgiving when forgiveness appears to be undeserved?

If you are like most people, the answer is *sometimes*, but not always, and actually, not nearly enough. Batting .300 is great in baseball, but not so good when it comes to treating those who agitate you with kindness and respect.

Our faith requires a much higher batting average, perhaps best achieved by approaching these situations as a team player. In other words, urge those around you to take the high road and not get sucked in by negative energy. By encouraging others, no doubt your own level of play will also be elevated.

.

"The purpose of life is a life of purpose."

-- Robert Byrne, author

The Game Clock is Ticking

Great games are not remembered by the stats or score. Instead, we remember the players and coaches, the attitudes and demeanors, the mistakes, and the miracle plays. The combination of all the game's components is what marks it for the ESPN highlight reel.

It is the same with our lives as well. Awards, titles and accomplishments are great, but they are really just like a long list of stats. God does not read the stat sheet. Instead, He looks at what we did throughout a lifetime, and the ripple effect we had on others. This thought can be encouraging to those who have spent their entire lives dedicated to doing God's work. But many of us may have entered the game late and wonder if there is enough time on the clock to make a difference in this world.

The point is, you don't know how much time is left on your game clock. Surely at some point, time expires, and you meet your Creator. But the period between now and then could be a matter of days, or a matter of decades. Even if you only have a day, that is still plenty of time to do something for God that benefits others.

"You never know that God is all you need until God is all you've got."

-- Rick Warren, pastor, author

Practice Drill for Trust

You probably know who Tony Dungy is. He is the former Super Bowl Champion coach for the Indianapolis Colts.

You may also know that Tony Dungy experienced great personal tragedy when in 2005, his 18 year-old son Jamie took his own life. The way Tony Dungy handled this terrible event can teach us something *so much* more important than the X's and O's of football. Because after Jamie died, Tony Dungy truly trusted God to heal him and his family, and to bring some good from this tragic situation.

Of course anyone familiar with football knows that well prepared football teams must practice hard. Well, Coach Dungy says that trusting God when something awful occurs requires practice as well. He says the practice drill for handling life's really difficult challenges is trusting God with your smaller setbacks, because then you are prepared to receive His grace and healing when life inevitably gets very, very tough.

"Life is 10% what happens to you, and 90% how you respond to it."

-- Lou Holtz, renowned college football coach

Universal Response

How do you react when something goes wrong in your life? You are probably thinking that it depends on what went wrong. That may be true, but there is a universal response that can apply in every difficult situation. The response does not involve asking why, placing blame, or trying to immediately fix things. It simply involves asking two questions: *What can I learn from this?* and *How does God want me to respond?*

That may sound easy, but as first hand experience will reveal, it is not. Our first response is often to react, or to try to fix, or to just be overwhelmed by emotion. Regardless of whether you have days or weeks to respond to a situation, or only a matter of moments, pausing to ask yourself these two questions will very often trigger a different response. And whatever it was that was about to engulf or enrage you will suddenly begin to lose its grip.

"Everybody is unique. Compare not yourself with anybody else lest you spoil God's curriculum."

-- Baal Shem Tov, Jewish sage

Antidote to Envy

Envy. We have all felt it from time to time, and it is a terrible feeling. It consumes your thoughts, eats you up inside, makes you unappreciative of what you have, and robs you of happiness. We all know what envy is, we all hate the feeling, but what can we do about it?

Professor Lawrence Cunningham from the University of Notre Dame says that while there is no sure cure for envy, if you could concoct a spiritual medicine for it, it would include these ingredients: an appreciation of your limits and capabilities, a more generous attitude toward others, a discipline of showing gratitude, and a greater sense of what ultimately matters in life.

Unfortunately you can't run down to your local drugstore and buy this medicine, but you can keep all the ingredients in stock – not in your medicine cabinet, but in your heart. And then when those feelings of resentment, bitterness and discontent start to surface, you will have exactly what you need to cure them.

"Humility does not mean thinking less of yourself than of other people, nor does it mean having a low opinion of your own gifts. It means freedom from thinking about yourself at all."

-- William Temple, Archbishop of York and Canterbury

Ego: Negative or Necessary?

Ego. Doesn't that word conjure up some awful images in your mind? But let's challenge some of those images. As many spiritual leaders will attest, nobody does anything great without a strong ego.

Think about Mother Theresa. She had a huge ego, a powerful self-image that allowed her to stand before the world, convinced of her worth.

Huge ego? You bet. And yet she was humble, actually a model of humility. How can that be? How could she have a huge ego while at the same time be the epitome of humility? Because she was always aware that everything that made her special and powerful did not come from her, but came from God.

Do not be paralyzed by inhibitions that prevent you from doing the great work you were sent here to do. God wants to work through you. Make a habit of keeping that thought front and center, and get to work.

"The ultimate measure of a man is not where he stands in moments of comfort and convenience, but where he stands at times of challenge and controversy."

-- Martin Luther King, Jr.

Twelve Step Program

If you think the 12 Step Program is only for alcoholics or drug addicts, think again! The program is a spiritual process. It essentially requires a person to admit to having a problem, acknowledge the need for God's help, and make amends for hurting others. According to Richard Rohr, a renowned spiritual thinker, the Twelve Step Program applies in each of our lives, and here's why:

We all have *addictions* to some sort of personal flaw. Maybe yours is anger, maybe your child is selfish, perhaps your spouse is unforgiving, maybe your co-worker is judgmental. We each have a flaw that no matter how hard we try, we just cannot shake it. If you apply the Twelve Steps to your flaw, you can minimize its impact. But more importantly, your life can be transformed, much like an alcoholic or drug addict's life is transformed. This kind of life altering transformation, after all, is essentially why God sent you here.

"He who dares not offend cannot be honest."

-- Thomas Paine, U.S. Founding Father

Conversations That Count

Long before Tony Dungy became a renowned NFL football coach, he was an undrafted walk-on with the Pittsburgh Steelers. He survived his first season, but going into his second season, he got very sick and started to despair over the likelihood of keeping his spot on the team. Five time Pro Bowl safety, Donnie Shell, pulled him aside and said, "Tony, you claim to put God first and to trust Him with your life, but as soon as something goes wrong, you panic and act as though everything depends on you making this team."

Tony Dungy says that comment was a turning point in his life because it taught him what it means to put God first and trust Him with your life. That message is important, but what is also important, is the idea that Donnie Shell had the courage to have that conversation in the first place.

It is often uncomfortable to talk with others about trusting God, but that is exactly what we need to do for each other. There are probably people in your life right now who are despairing over something. Perhaps all they need is for someone like you to have a similar conversation with them.

"The weak can never forgive. Forgiveness is an attribute of the strong."

-- Gandhi

No Extra Credit

Forgiveness is hard work, and it is easy to be resentful of the effort required on your part when you weren't the one that did something wrong. When you feel indignant about the effort you have to exert, you should remember two things:

First, God requires you to forgive. Forgiveness is not about scoring extra credit points on the test – it *is* the test. If you don't forgive, you fail the test.

Second, remember when you pass the test by doing all the hard work required to forgive someone else, *you* are the one that reaps the benefits. You are rewarded in *this life* by the feeling of peace that replaces the anger and hurt you harbored. More importantly, you are rewarded in *eternal life* because God will in turn forgive you for the transgressions you have committed.

God's forgiveness and mercy may be His greatest gift to you. Do not underestimate the importance of sharing this gift with others.

"Of course God knows best what we need, but it is slothful to leave the initiative to Him. We must knock at the door -- and often."

– David Yount, author, columnist, former White House correspondent

Waiting for You to Ask

How often do you ask God for help? How many times did you ask Him today? Yesterday? If you are facing a difficult period in your life, you may frequently ask for His help. But what if your life is pretty good right now? Do you still ask for help throughout your day?

You do not need to make an appointment, dial a phone, or send an email or text. All you have to do is clear your mind for a moment and ask for His help. God's assistance is literally just a *thought* away, so why not seek it?

Is it because you do not feel your need is worthy of God's intervention? Is it because you feel you should be able to accomplish it on your own? Or did it simply not occur to you to ask?

Know that God is with you all day long. You have His undivided attention. He wants you to talk to Him. He wants to give you advice. But sometimes, God is just waiting for you to ask.

"We don't invent our mission, we detect it."

-- Victor Frankl, Holocaust survivor

Laboratory of Our Souls

No two individuals have the same DNA, so DNA is often used to confirm a person's identity. But there is another way to distinguish individuals from each other. This technique does not occur in a scientific laboratory, but rather in the laboratory called *our souls*.

A laboratory is a place where knowledge is pondered, assumptions are tested and learning takes place. Those are exactly the kinds of activities you must pursue deep in your soul so you can identify the unique package God placed within you: a distinct combination of strengths, limitations and passions, that once you understand, will reveal the specific work God needs you to do.

You have a God-given nature. You need to discover and respond to that nature rather than responding to all the external pressures and demands that want to steer you in a different direction. Listen to that voice deep within, and then follow what you hear.

"The people we surround ourselves with either raise or lower our standards. No man becomes great on his own. No woman becomes great on her own. The people around them help make them great."

-- Matthew Kelly, author, speaker

Who Surrounds You?

The founder of a large homeless shelter once said that a recovering addict cannot possibly maintain sobriety if he or she is surrounded by people who are still using. Likewise, you cannot be the person God created you to be if you are surrounded solely by people of lukewarm faith leading complacent lives of relative comfort.

No matter how great your intentions are to be the person God wants you to be, you cannot make it as a lone ranger. The answer is not in the *number* of faith-filled, inspiring people you find, but rather it lies in the authenticity of their example. Find those people in your life; they are there. They are in your workplace, in your community, in your school; they are everywhere. God has seen to it that there are people in your life who *you* can relate to. People who will challenge you when you need to be pushed, and will support you when you need to be picked up. Now go tip your hand a bit, and find them.

"Never be afraid to trust an unknown future to a known God."

– Corrie ten Boom, Dutch Christian who helped Jews escape the Nazi Holocaust

Left to Tell

In 1994, a terrible genocide swept through the country of Rwanda resulting in the horrendous deaths of millions of innocent people. Throughout this three-month holocaust, a young college student named Immaculee Ilibagiza hid with six other women in a tiny bathroom. She entered the bathroom as a 5'9 115 pound young woman, and emerged as an emaciated 65 pound survivor, only to find that her family members had been gruesomely dismembered and killed by government-sponsored evil.

God did not simply choose Immaculee to survive among the millions that perished. She survived because she chose God. She chose to turn to Him, trust Him and do His will. Because of the choices Immaculee made about her relationship with God, she was left to tell her story for others. If God could guide Immaculee through this ordeal, do you have any doubt He can sustain you in your trials and tribulations? The answer lies in *you* choosing God.

"Each day of our lives we make deposits in the memory banks of our children."

– Charles Swindoll, pastor, author, radio show personality

Parents as Leaders

It is astounding how often kids leave other kids out. But even more astounding is how often parents observe, but ignore, the exclusion.

Every time a young person is excluded by other kids, it of course chips away at that person's self-esteem. But do not think for a second that it is not chipping away at the kids who are doing the ignoring or excluding. It may not be chipping away at their self-esteem, but it is taking huge chunks out of that thing inside of them called *character*.

And what about the effect on the parents who remain silent? Every time you ignore a character flaw in your child, or simply look the other way, you are chipping away at your own character as well.

Your kids are most certainly going to make mistakes with regard to character. But those mistakes provide their greatest opportunities to learn. As a parent, you have to seize these teaching moments. You owe it to your kids, and you owe it to God.

"Life's most persistent and urgent question is, 'What are you doing for others?'"

-- Martin Luther King, Jr.

Analogy for Service

When it comes to serving others, have you ever wondered what you should do, how much you should do, or how you should do it? A useful analogy for answering these questions might be looking at how parents serve their children:

Do parents do only big and important things for their kids? Of course not. Much of what they do are small, seemingly insignificant things. Yet, in the eyes of their kids, these small things are often just as important as the big ones.

Do parents do *everything* they would like to do for their kids? No. But they do the necessary things, and then they do as many other things as they are capable of doing.

And finally, how do parents serve their kids? They serve their children in a loving way, with patience, kindness and selflessness, and with no need for special recognition.

The point is to think about serving others in a way that resembles how you serve your family: by doing things that are both big and small, taking advantage of every opportunity you can, and doing so for no other reason than to show love to others.

"In a culture of confusion and in a world of constant change, many people don't have a spiritual North Star, which is what God's dream for us provides."

— Matthew Kelly, author, speaker

Sustainment

What is it that you count on when something is going badly in your life? The fact that you have a great marriage? Good friends? Financial security?

If you have *any* of these blessings, no doubt they can provide much needed support when life gets tough. But they should not be your ultimate source of strength, and here's why:

Every one of these blessings can disappear in an instant. Healthy people can suddenly become ill. Husbands, wives, kids, and friends -- they can be unexpectedly taken from you. And your life long savings can disappear in a financial crisis.

You get the picture. Everything important and sustaining in your life can disappear very quickly. Everything, except one thing. The one thing that can provide peace, understanding and love, and that can never be taken away is your relationship with God. The key is to start trusting Him now with your minor challenges. Then you will be able to find Him when you need Him for the big one.

"Serenity is not freedom from the storm, but calmness within the storm."

-- Unknown

Diluting Negative Influences

No one can withstand our culture's constant barrage of negative influences without being personally affected. Your sense of right and wrong starts to blur. Your standards start to drop. What you previously thought was awful begins to feel *normal*.

You cannot avoid all the negative influences around you, but you can *dilute* these influences by seeking to fill your life with positive things. Immorality affects your soul like junk food affects your body. A little junk food is inevitable and isn't going to harm you as long as you are giving your body a steady stream of healthy and nutritious food.

Likewise, seeking positive influences in your life (such as good people, inspiring books and music, and uplifting experiences) serves to proactively counteract the negativism that surrounds you. And instead of getting dragged down by the culture, you may even start to steer it ever so slightly in a new, positive direction.

"If a man does not keep pace with his companions, perhaps it is because he hears a different drummer."

-- David Thoreau, author, philosopher

Expectations

Most people would say a nice person is thoughtful, considerate and kind. But many people fail to realize that a person's ability to regularly demonstrate these characteristics is often due to circumstances he or she does not control.

C.S. Lewis, in his landmark book *Mere Christianity*, described how a person's physical conditions form the foundation of their temperament. Advances in medicine have confirmed what C.S. Lewis said. People whose brains and hormones are balanced are often nice, *very* nice. And if they were being honest, they would admit that being nice is not that difficult. On the other hand, people whose brains and bodies do not function as intended often lack self-control, self-confidence, and even friends.

Don't let the hand you were dealt lead to self-righteousness, nor self-condemnation. And just as importantly, don't presume to know the hands dealt to others.

"One of the greatest threats to faith is busyness. It's jumping from one thing to another, and therefore never developing the prayerful/contemplative side of our lives sufficiently so that we might hear God."

-- Lou Nanni, VP, University of Notre Dame

Ignoring God?

If you have spent a fair amount of time around children or teens, you for sure know how difficult it can be to get their attention. When they have their eyes glued to a computer or TV screen, you can repeat yourself, you can raise your voice, you can probably even wave your arms in front of their face, and you still may not get their attention! Have you ever wondered if God is getting the same reaction from you?

If you can't hear God, you will experience spiritual suffocation. You will miss the opportunity to grow in wisdom, and you will never grasp what you ultimately seek, which is real peace, deep within, that can only come from God.

Undoubtedly your life is busy, but how about trying to carve out three minutes of silence each day with no distractions and a clear mind. Commit to doing that for a week. If you do, God *will* get your attention. And once He does, you'll begin to see, hear and experience life in a whole new way.

"As long as we continue to live as if we are what we do, what we have, and what other people think about us, we will remain filled with judgments, opinions, and condemnations."

– Henri Nouwen, author, professor, priest

Identity

Have you ever given thought to how you define yourself? Your definition matters because it affects your sense of self-worth.

Some of us define ourselves by what we do. When we are successfully doing the things we do in life, we feel effective and worthy. But when we start to fail, insecurity creeps in.

Some of us define ourselves by what others say about us. When people speak highly of us, we feel great. But we are apt to get upset and defensive when people criticize and judge us.

Finally, many of us define ourselves by what we have, which leads us to fall apart when we lose whatever it is that we think is so critical to who we are.

The problem with all of these identities is that they eventually lead to self-rejection. To avoid self-rejection, identify yourself first and foremost as a son or daughter of God. This definition inspires you to figure out who *God* intends you to become, which in turn leads to the kind of fulfillment that no job, possession or other person can give you.

"There are difference makers in every game, and there are difference makers in life. I don't believe we should try to fit in and be like everyone else. I believe we all have to step out and do our part."

-- Mike Babcock, NHL Stanley Cup Champion and Olympic Gold Medal Hockey Coach

Morality

Morality is one of those words that can be difficult to define. Morality is not just about following rules, it is not just about avoiding sin, and it is not just about being nice.

Morality entails using your God-given gifts to do God's work – and there is plenty of work God needs you to do: in your family, in your workplace and among your friends. Your soul is indelibly marked by your daily decisions to work (or not work) on God's behalf.

Being nice is not enough. Neither is focusing on only one or two big efforts. Your decision to defend a ridiculed co-worker this morning can be just as significant as the 50 hours you spent volunteering at the local soup kitchen last year.

Remember: God knows your individual capabilities. He knows if you are stretching yourself, and He knows if you are not.

"The right to do something does not mean that doing it is right."

-- William Saffire, Pulitzer Prize winner and long time NY Times columnist

Fair or Right?

In the late 1960's, my father-in-law, Bill Guilfoile, was named Public Relations Director for the Pittsburgh Pirates. On his first day on the job, a well-known sports writer requested Bill to set up an interview with Roberto Clemente. Bill approached Clemente, introduced himself, and relayed the interview request.

Clemente reacted with a passionate three-minute outburst! He obviously had had a major falling out with the writer, which everyone, except the new PR director, knew. Clemente, perhaps rightly so, felt the sports writer did not deserve an interview after what he had previously done to Clemente. But when you focus on giving people what they deserve, you can lose sight of doing what is right.

Clemente's rant ended, he regained his composure, and asked Bill if it would help if he did the interview. Bill said it would, and Roberto said, "Then I will do it," and he did.

Is there someone in your life who does not deserve all you can potentially give? Seek them out and give them something they don't deserve. It may not change them, but it will likely change you.

"The reason leaders fail often has little to do with their professional capabilities. The reason many leaders fail is because something in their personal and spiritual life is not quite right."

-- Tony Dungy, Super Bowl Champion Coach

Doing & Accomplishing

It is easy to get way too focused on what you do and accomplish. And if you are a parent, it is really easy to get caught up in what your kids do and accomplish. This is especially true if your kids are in high school and will soon be completing those college applications that want to know all about their achievements. Think about how much time you spend talking to your kids about schoolwork, grades, their sports or activities, and perhaps getting their chores done.

Without question, these efforts are important – you certainly do not want your kids just sitting around all day. And encouraging them to work hard and do their best will certainly help them in life. But are grades, activities and responsibilities all they should be focusing on? Of course not, but if these are the things you talk about most, these will be the things they will think are most important. And the kinds of things that are ultimately important, the kinds of things that strengthen the condition of their souls, will be an after-thought at best.

"Everybody can be great, because anybody can serve. You only need a heart full of grace; a soul generated by love."

– Martin Luther King, Jr.

Service Versus Leadership

Can you imagine attending a leadership presentation, and the first thing the speaker says to you is don't seek to be a leader? If Lou Nanni, VP of the University of Notre Dame, is the speaker, that is exactly what you might hear. Lou, who is frequently asked to give talks about leadership, often shocks the person who invited him to speak because he begins his speech by saying, *"Don't seek to be leaders. Instead seek to be servants."* Not exactly what you would expect to hear, but there is tremendous value in that thought.

Often when a person seeks leadership, what is really driving them is their own internal gratification, or their need to climb some sort of corporate or social ladder. Instead, if you seek to serve others purely and abundantly -- whether it be your family, your friends, people who report to you at work, people in your community -- leadership will be given to you. And leadership is always better when it is *given* rather than when it is *sought*.

"Peace and joy can come to us only when we stop demanding that life — our spouses, our families, our friends, our vocations and vacations — give us something that they cannot give, namely, the finished symphony, clear-cut joy, complete consummation."

-- Ron Rolheiser, author, speaker, priest

Taming Our Restlessness

Restlessness is like an undertow in the ocean. It is almost always present, sometimes raging forcefully, other times it just nags at you, and every once in a while, it momentarily disappears, but usually not for long.

Why do you so often feel the undertow of restlessness? Isn't your life full with work, family and other worthwhile efforts? Are you just being greedy and selfish when this feeling surfaces?

Most spiritual leaders would say restlessness is part of your human condition, because you were created with an infinite spirit. So does that mean you just have to live with this feeling? To some degree, yes, but there are ways to tame it. Giving in to the urge to seek more activity is *not* one of those ways because it only serves to fan the flames of restlessness. Instead, seek solitude and quiet. It is in those moments of silence and introspection that your restlessness can be comfortably contained.

"Communicating with God is like listening to the radio; there is always something to hear, but we must turn it on."

-- David Yount, author, columnist, former White House correspondent

Messages from God

Many people say that when they ask for God's help, He doesn't respond. Maybe they don't know how God answers.

God's help comes in many different forms. Sometimes it comes in the form of an insight. Sometimes it is just an inner feeling you get. Very often, it comes through the words and actions of other people. You first need to recognize these events for what they are -- support and direction from God. Then you have to do your part, which is being open to them, reflecting on them, and most importantly, *allowing them to alter your thinking.*

Of course not every inner feeling, nor every word spoken, will be a message from God. Some instincts create fear, and some people do and say things that hurt rather than help. But these are not God's messages. You can recognize God's messages from the peaceful, comforting or insightful perspective they provide.

"Nothing can be more useful to a man than a determination not to be hurried."

— David Thoreau, author, philosopher

Think What You Think

We live in a world of constant communication. Your smart phone, iPad and laptop give you instant access to news, music, TV, online shopping, even friends. Almost everything you want is literally at your fingertips. You can be amused, distracted, and catered to 24/7. And while your life may be super efficient, are you in danger of being attentive to so many things that, ultimately, you are not being attentive to anything?

One thing technology cannot give you is depth. And so you have to know when it is time to turn off the phone, shut down the computer, and even resist going out for coffee with a friend, so that, for a few moments at least, you can think what you really think, and know what you instinctively know. Try it. You might be surprised at how enlightening and engaging it is.

"All their life in this world had only been the cover and title page; now they were beginning Chapter 1 of the Great Story, which no one on earth has read, which goes on forever, and which every chapter is better than the one before."

-- C.S. Lewis on the last page of The Chronicles of Narnia

What Are You Living For?

Your thoughts about death can have a big influence on how you approach life. You can live your life as if it is all you have, as if death is an ending that has no bearing on how you live. Or, you can choose to trust that death is the sometimes painful, but blessed passage that will bring you face-to-face with God. People in the latter category, who have this unshakeable trust, tend to live their lives differently than those who don't. It is not that they live their lives passively, as if waiting for what is to come. Quite the opposite as they live it with more passion and fulfillment because they *know* what awaits them.

Here is an analogy: imagine two sports teams, each holding separate practices on nearby fields. One team knows it is playing in the championship that weekend: the other team's season is over once practice ends. It's obvious which team will practice with more excitement and commitment.

And so it is with your life as well. Your life on earth will be more fulfilling when you trust something great is awaiting you.

"Silence in the face of evil is itself evil. God will not hold us guiltless. Not to speak is to speak. Not to act is to act."

-- Dietrich Bonheoffer, theologian, martyr in German Resistance Movement

Do More

Do you ever struggle with wanting to do the right thing, but at the same time, you don't want to create a difficult situation? For example, you have probably at times been around people who are judgmental or critical of your values. You may have also watched friends or family members making bad choices. How many times have you opted not to speak up because you do not want to deal with the repercussions if you did?

Each of us, when faced with situations that require courage, no doubt have had some regrets. We have probably all looked the other way at times when we should have stood strong. But some of us succumb to social pressure so often that it no longer feels uncomfortable.

You have to work hard to become the type of person who does the right thing despite pressure to do otherwise. Strengthening your soul is like strengthening your body. You need steady and demanding exercise to strengthen your body. Likewise, you must consistently make tough choices if you want to strengthen your *soul*.

ABOUT THE AUTHOR

Prior to launching Everyday Faith, Shari Guilfoile had a 20-year consulting career where she worked with the management teams of many Fortune 100 companies. Shari was often chosen to pitch new ideas or insights because she had a knack for anticipating what an audience was thinking, and then describing ideas in a way that would resonate with those to whom she was speaking. She now uses those same gifts, but for a much greater purpose: to provide meaningful ways of looking at faith that attract and inspire people, no matter where they stand on their spiritual path. After receiving degrees from the University of Notre Dame and the University of Michigan, and after living most of their lives in the Midwest, Shari and her husband Pete moved with their three teenage children to Northern California in 2009.